GETTING STARTED

By Wally Kappelmann

You are about to embark on an exciting journey through the world of music. By following this playing guide and using the fun-features on your keyboard, you'll be playing real music in just a short time.

While this material can be applied to any keyboard instrument, it's aimed mainly at the new single keyboards with automatic bass. Since the book is general in nature, you'll want your owner's guide handy should you need to clarify various features mentioned in the following pages.

CONTENTS

ISBN 0-7935-0806-1
Previously: ISBN 0-88704-087-X

HAL•LEONARD®
CORPORATION
7777 W. BLUEMOUND RD. P.O. BOX 13819 MILWAUKEE, WI 53213

Sound Set-ups (Registration)

As you play songs in this book, you'll see such markings as Full 'N' Mellow, etc. The chart below will help you match the voices you have with the Sound Set-Ups shown on various pages.

SOFT SOLO	BRILLIANT SOLO	FULL 'N' BRILLIANT	FULL 'N' MELLOW	BRIGHT 'N' BRASSY	BIG 'N' BOLD	CLASSICAL
(Play single-note melodies)		(Play melody along with right-hand chords)			(single notes or chords, depending on instrument)	
Celeste/Music Box	Accordion	Accordion	Clarinet	Brass/Brass Ensemble	Flute	Chime
Cello	Bagpipe	Bandoneon	Flute/Tibia	Fluegelhorn	Guitar	Clavichord
Clarinet	Bandoneon	Organ	Horn	Synthe Brass	Organ	Guitar
Flute/Tibia	Banjo	Saxophone	Organ	Trombone	Piano	Harpsichord
Guitar	Calliope	String Ensemble	Piano/Elec. Piano	Trumpet	Saxophone	Piano
Harmonica	Fluegelhorn	Violin/String	Trombone			Pipe Organ
Harp	Glockenspiel (or Bells)					String Ensemble
Horn	Harpsichord					Violin/String
Marimba	Koto					
Piano/Elec. Piano	Mandolin					
Recorder	Oboe					
Trombone	Reed					
Vibraphone (Vibes)	Saxophone					
	Trumpet					
	Violin/String					
	Xylophone					

Depending on specific voices on your instrument, you'll have to decide which categories include various synthesized voices having non-instrumental names. "Space Wah," for example, could resemble a guitar — or a trumpet — or neither. The best thing to do is to try the sound and add it to the above chart wherever you think it should go.

To get you started on your first song, use the following set-up for your solo, or melody voice:
FLUTE or TIBIA 8
VIBRATO
REVERB (if you have it): Medium
NOTE: On some keyboards, the flute tabs are labelled "tibia." The two names are interchangeable.

If you want to learn all about Sound Set-Ups — such as which sounds go with which songs — see "Creating Sounds On Your Electronic Keyboard," another book in the Creative Playing Series. Now it's possible to learn the HOW and WHY of registration. This book offers easy guidelines in a clear, straightforward style. See you dealer for your copy.

Song 1: Lightly Row

Playing Melodies

The melody is played by your right hand. Melodies are made up of specific musical sounds. To represent these sounds, notes are placed on a *STAFF*, as shown in Figure A. The staff consists of five lines and four spaces and each is named with one of the letters A through G. Any note that appears on one of the lines or in one of the spaces is called by that letter-name.

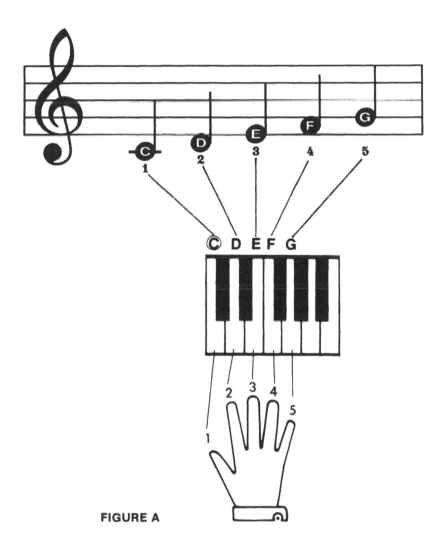

FIGURE A

The S-shaped symbol at the beginning of the staff is call the *TREBLE CLEF* and tells you all the notes that follow are to be played by your right hand.

Also illustrated are the first five melody notes, C, D, E, F, and G and their corresponding keys. To help you play the notes with your right hand, numbers are placed above or alongside each note telling you which finger to use.

Place your right hand on the keys with your thumb on *MIDDLE C* as shown in Figure A. As a learning aid in this book, middle C is circled in all keyboard illustrations.

Play the following melodies. They're parts of well-known songs and will give you practice in using the first five melody notes. If the tunes are familiar to you, try to play them as you know them, or hear them in your mind. As a helpful hint, hold the white notes a little longer than the black notes — we'll talk more about this later. Relax and keep your fingers close to the keys.

Marianne

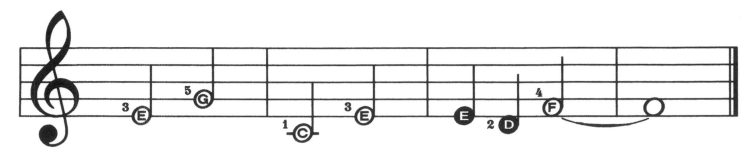

Hey Lolly, Lolly

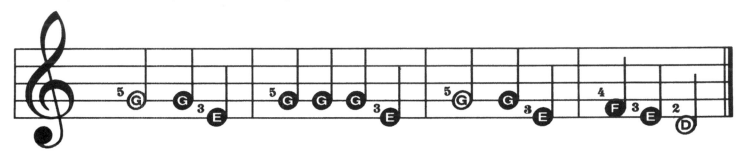

Merrily We Roll Along

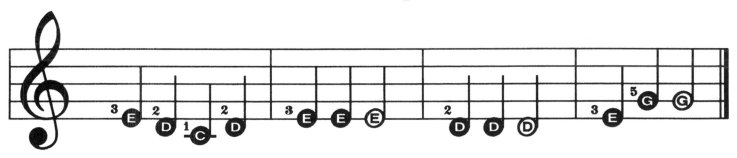

A-Tisket, A-Tasket

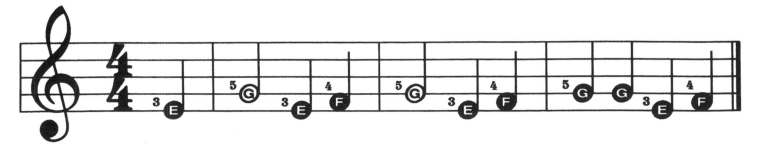

After you feel comfortable playing these melodies, play LIGHTLY ROW. Keep your fingers over the five keys and watch the music, not your hands.

Lightly Row

SOFT SOLO

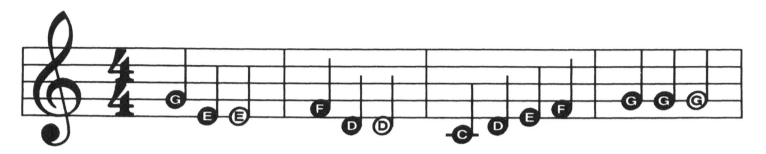

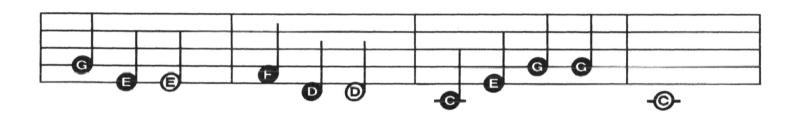

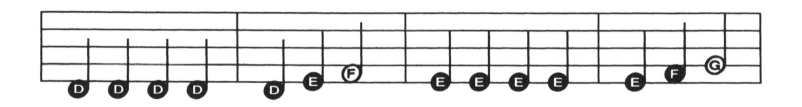

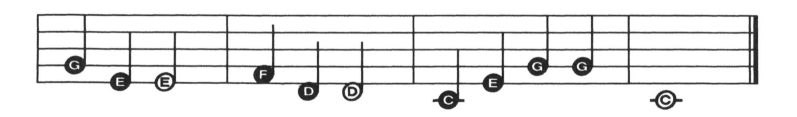

Song 2: Lightly Row

Playing Accompaniment

Accompaniment is the background for the melody. It usually consists of chords and bass tones. Chords are three or more tones played at the same time. They can be rhythmic or continuous, depending on your preference.

Most keyboards today have an easy-play accompaniment feature — one-finger, or similar — and that is the basis for this book.

Set up a flute or tibia voice for the accompaniment section of the keyboard.

Chord Symbols

Chords are represented in music by *CHORD SYMBOLS* which are small boxes containing letters. They appear above the melody in each song, as shown in Figure A, and they tell you which chord to play. For example, when the C symbol appears, you should play the C chord key in the accompaniment section. Each chord symbol remains in effect until you come to the next one.

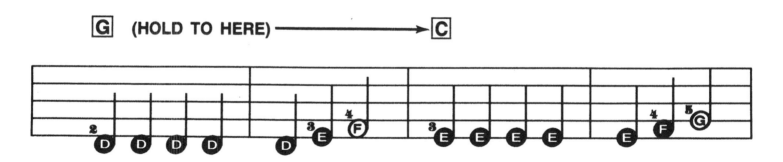

FIGURE A

The C and G Chords

The first two chords you'll use are the C and G MAJOR chords. They're shown in Figure B.

Easy-Play Chords

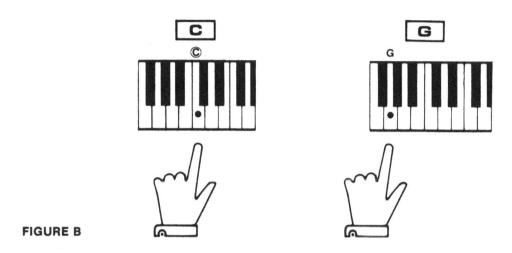

FIGURE B

If your keyboard has a memory feature, all you have to do is press and release the chord key which corresponds to the letter in the chord symbol box.

The chord and bass notes keep playing until you press another chord key.

Forming Your Own Chords

Figure C shows the notes of the C and G chords. Practice these chords, changing from one to the other, until you can do it easily.

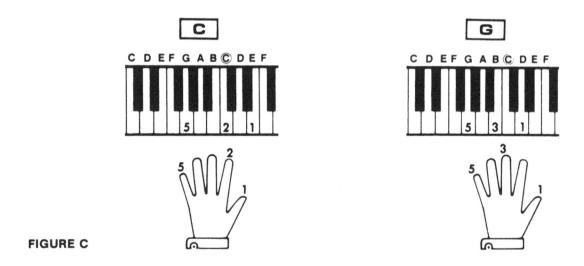

FIGURE C

Play LIGHTLY ROW, on the next page, this time adding the accompaniment indicated by the chord symbols.

It's a good idea to practice playing the song slowly at first and gradually increase the speed when you feel ready.

Lightly Row

SOFT SOLO

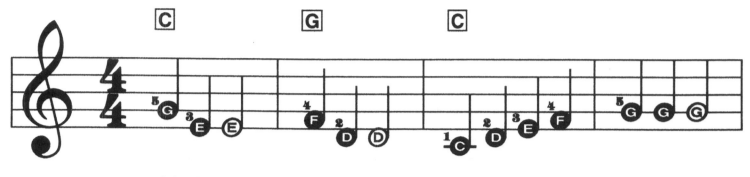

Light - ly row, light - ly row, o'er the glass - y waves we go;

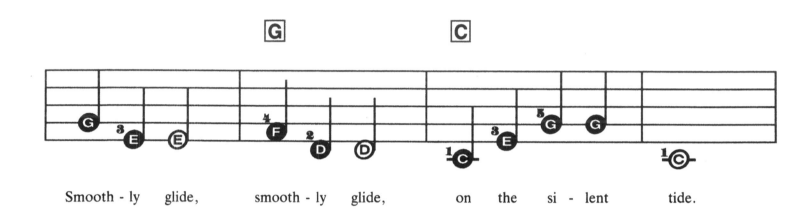

Smooth - ly glide, smooth - ly glide, on the si - lent tide.

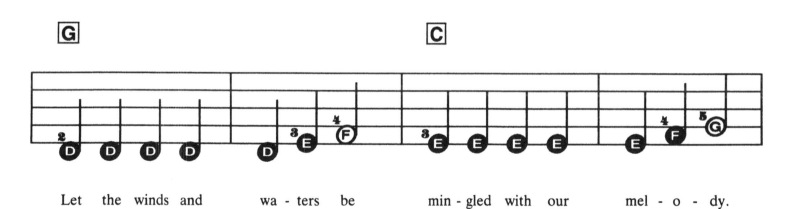

Let the winds and wa - ters be min - gled with our mel - o - dy.

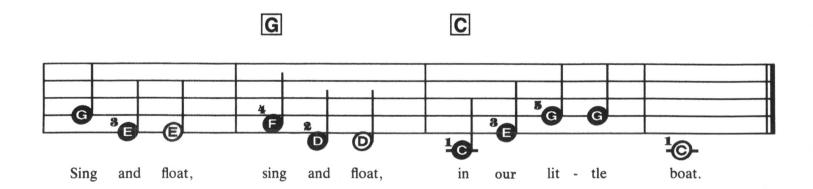

Sing and float, sing and float, in our lit - tle boat.

Song 3:
Long, Long Ago

A New Note

The note *A* is introduced in this song and is shown in Figure A. As you continue to learn new right hand melody notes, use the suggested fingering.

This will help you move out of the range of the first five notes without "running out of fingers."

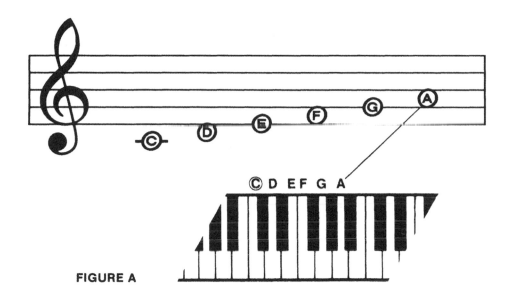

FIGURE A

Time Values

To have a good time playing the keyboard, all you really need to know about written music is that notes indicate

PITCH — The higher and lower tones that make up the melody of a song, and

TIME — How long notes are held. If you're playing by yourself, you may never have to think about counting; you'll just play what you "hear in your mind." Try to relate playing to walking; don't think about it — just do it. If it feels right, it probably is.

On the other hand . . .

Here are reasons you might want to know about time values:

1. To play unfamiliar songs (once learned, the above statements apply).

2. To play with other musicians (who also don't think about time values).

In either of these events, 1). look over Figure B, 2.) tap your foot and play the notes, and 3.) immediately put time values out of your mind.

FIGURE B

WHOLE NOTE
4 beats

HALF NOTE
2 beats

QUARTER NOTE
1 beat

Rest assured that the more you play, as in anything, the easier it becomes. Eventually, you'll play a new song and, even though time values are

in your mind, you won't consciously think about them. You'll just play — and enjoy.

Measures

Figure C illustrates how the staff is divided into equal sections by using vertical lines called *BAR LINES*. The sections between the bar lines are called *MEASURES*.

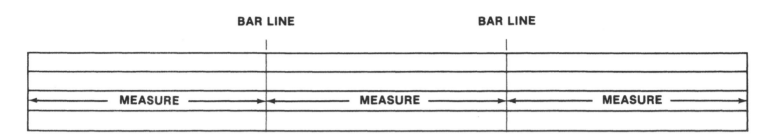

FIGURE C

Time Signature

The two numbers at the beginning of a song are known as the *TIME SIGNATURE*. The top number indicates the number of beats in each measure. The bottom number tells you the type of note that receives one beat. In Figure D, the bottom number 4 indicates each quarter note receives one beat. The song LONG, LONG AGO has a 4/4 time signature.

FIGURE D

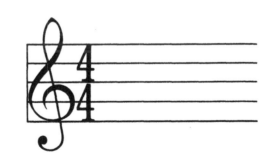

Play LONG, LONG AGO. A HELPFUL HINT: When learning a new song, play just the melody at a slow, even speed. Once you can play it comfortably and without hesitation, add the chords and gradually increase the speed.

If you tap your foot, play the melody with the foot taps, rather than tap your foot in time with the notes. This will better prepare you for playing with automatic rhythm.

Long, Long Ago

CLASSICAL

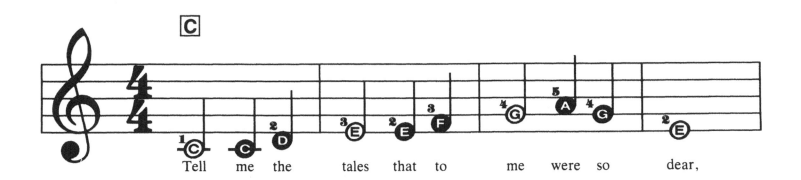

Tell   me   the   tales   that   to   me   were   so   dear,

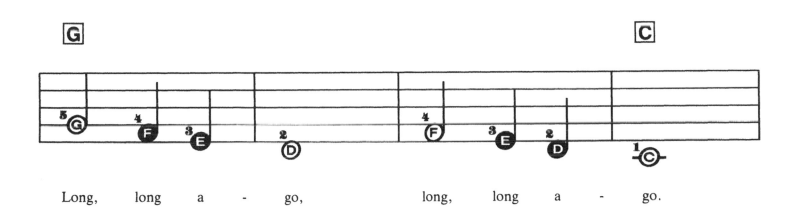

Long,   long   a -   go,   long,   long   a -   go.

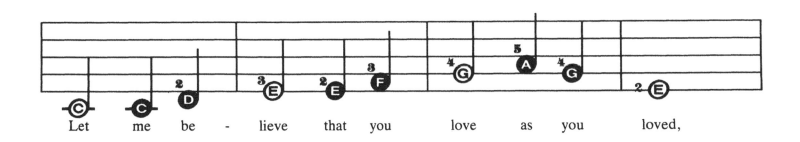

Let   me   be -   lieve   that   you   love   as   you   loved,

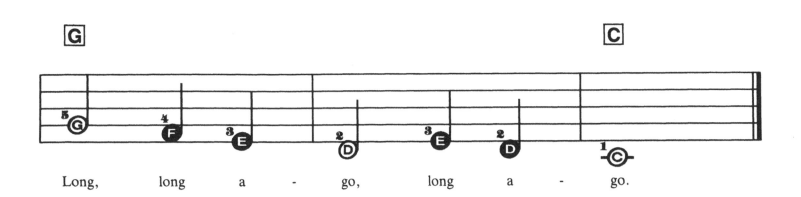

Long,   long   a -   go,   long   a -   go.

Song 4: Marianne

A New Note

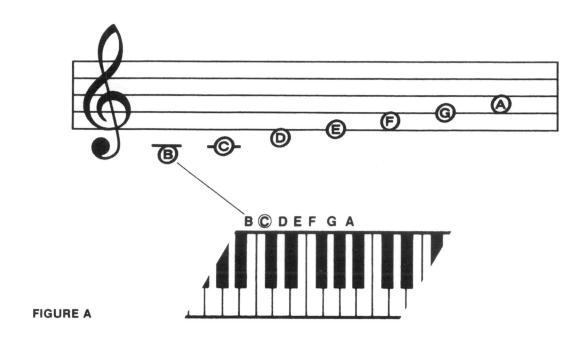

FIGURE A

Ties

A curved line connecting two notes on the same line or in the same space is called a *TIE*. A tie indicates that the first note should be played and then held for the total time value of both notes. Because only the first note is struck, the notes following have no letter-names inside.

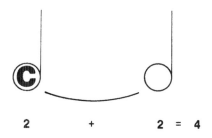

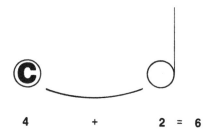

Playing With Rhythm

Here are some guidelines to help you play along with the automatic rhythm.

1. Physically play the music without the rhythm. This involves locating the correct melody and chord keys, observing the suggested fingering, and incorporating any new musical information. Work toward doing it all without taking your eyes off the music.

2. Play the music mentally. This means read the music without playing. Try to "hear" the melody in your mind and imagine how each chord sounds as its symbol appears in the music. Humming the melody may help.

3. Watch the music and mentally play while the automatic rhythm is operating. As you "hear" the music in your mind, notice how it relates to the drum sounds.

4. Physically play the music along with the automatic rhythm. By this time, you'll really be familiar with what you're playing.

The 4/4 time signature was introduced in Lesson 3. Listen to a 4/4 drum rhythm — press the FOX TROT or SWING button in the rhythm section and press a chord key. You'll hear a repeating rhythm pattern of a heavy beat followed by a light beat. A portion of this pattern is shown in Figure C. As you listen to the rhythm, try to hear the melody of MARIANNE in your mind, provided you know the song.

FIGURE C

Since the time signature 4/4 indicates four beats to a measure, this pattern can be grouped into units of four beats. Each group has the heavy sound of the bass drum on the first and third beats and the lighter sound of the cymbal on the second and fourth beats. This rhythm pattern is sometimes referred to as BOOM-chick-BOOM-chick as illustrated in Figure D.

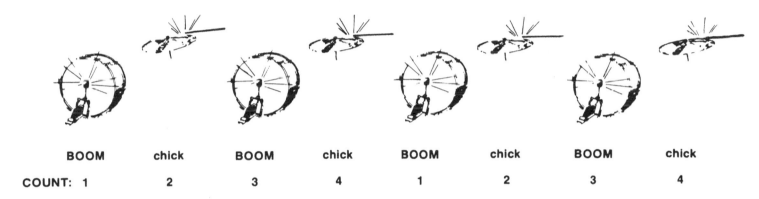

BOOM	chick	BOOM	chick	BOOM	chick	BOOM	chick
COUNT: 1	2	3	4	1	2	3	4

FIGURE D

As you hold the chord key, you'll also hear the deep sound of the bass being played on the first and third beats and the chords being played on the second and fourth beats as shown in Figure E.

COUNT: 1   2   3   4   1   2   3   4

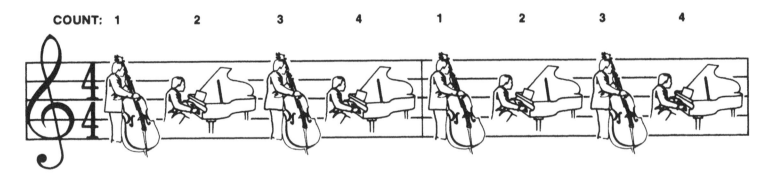

FIGURE E

From this point on, a rhythm setting is given for each song. Practice slowly at first and gradually increase the tempo as playing becomes easier.

Practice MARIANNE using the Fox Trot or Swing rhythm. Start slowly and gradually increase the tempo as you become more familiar with the music.

Marianne

Medium slow FOX TROT

FULL 'N' MELLOW

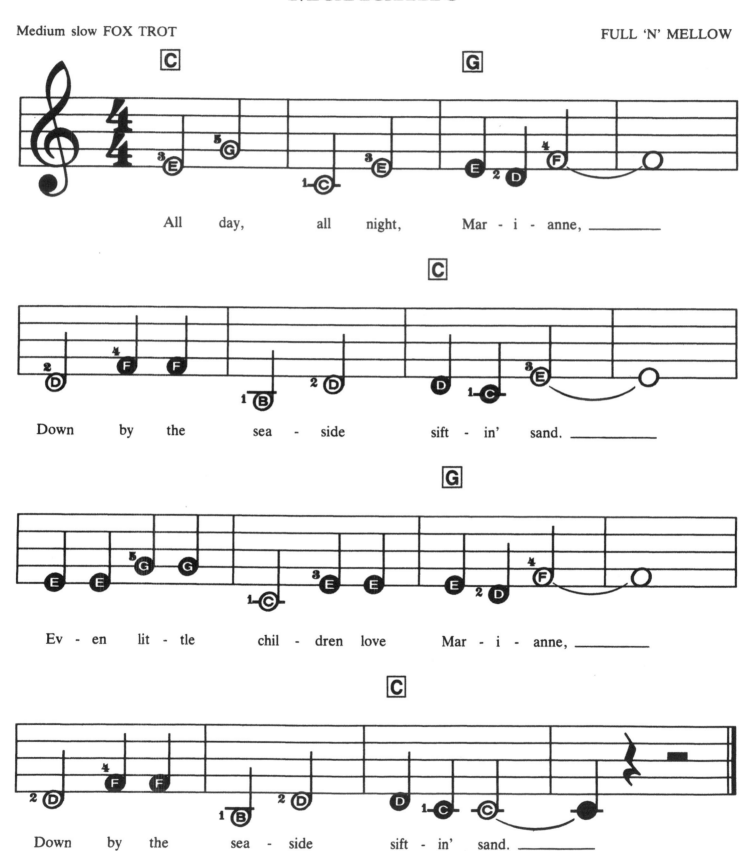

All day, all night, Mar - i - anne, _____

Down by the sea - side sift - in' sand. _____

Ev - en lit - tle chil - dren love Mar - i - anne, _____

Down by the sea - side sift - in' sand. _____

Song 5: Michael, Row the Boat Ashore

A New Chord

Easy-Play

FIGURE A

Forming Your Own Chords

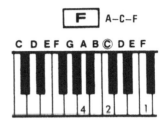

Pick-up Notes

Very often, a song starts with one or more notes whose time values do not total a complete measure. The notes in this incomplete measure are called *PICK-UP NOTES*. The missing beats are always found in the last measure of the song. In many cases, pick-up notes are played before an accompaniment chord is played.

The beginning and ending of MICHAEL, ROW THE BOAT ASHORE are shown in Figure B. The first two quarter notes total only two beats. The 4/4 time signature calls for four beats in each measure. The two beats missing from the first measure are found at the end of the song. Play the two pick-up notes before you play the chord.

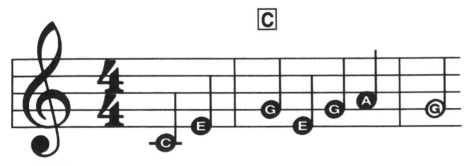

FIGURE B

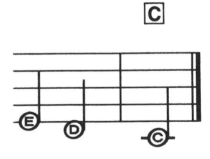

If your keyboard has a feature called Synchro-Start, this song is a good place to use it because of the pick-up notes. See your owner's manual.

Incidentally, the Creative Playing Series includes a book called "Exploring Automatic Features on Your Keyboard." Synchro-Start is just one of the many features discussed. See your dealer for a copy.

Michael, Row The Boat Ashore

Medium FOX TROT

BIG 'N' BOLD

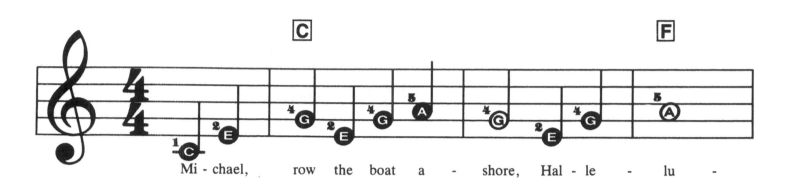

Mi - chael, row the boat a - shore, Hal - le - lu -

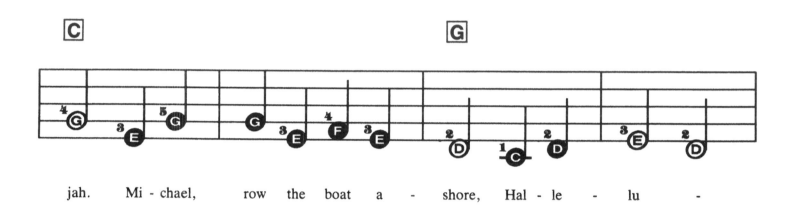

jah. Mi - chael, row the boat a - shore, Hal - le - lu -

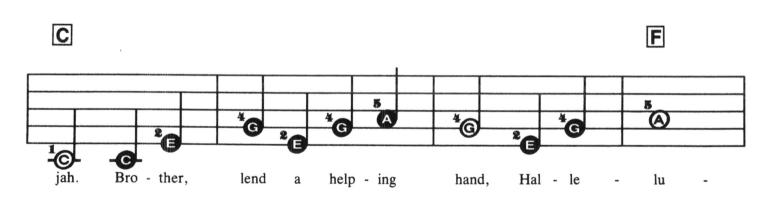

jah. Bro - ther, lend a help - ing hand, Hal - le - lu -

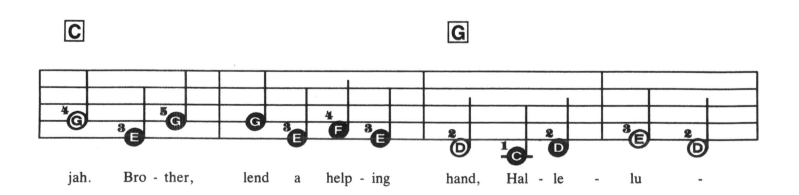

jah. Bro - ther, lend a help - ing hand, Hal - le - lu -

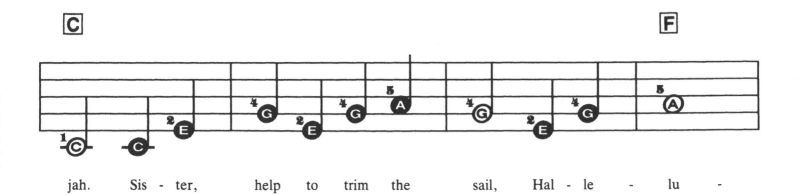

jah. Sis - ter, help to trim the sail, Hal - le - lu -

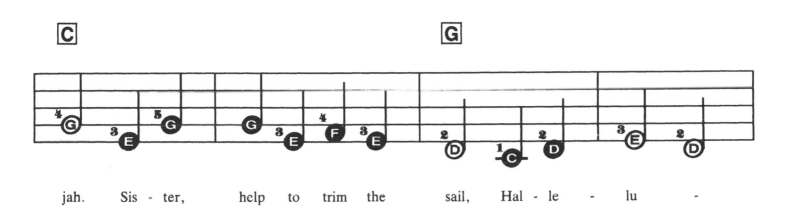

jah. Sis - ter, help to trim the sail, Hal - le - lu -

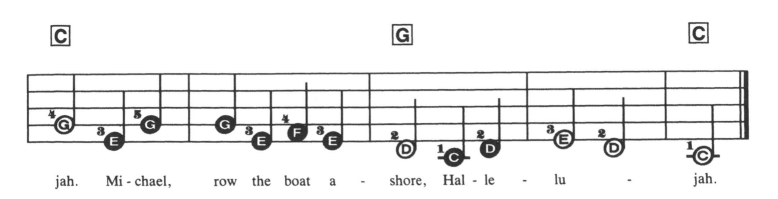

jah. Mi - chael, row the boat a - shore, Hal - le - lu -

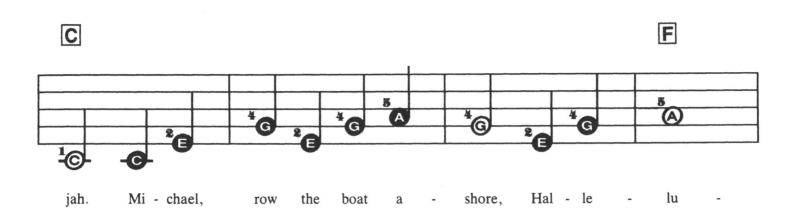

jah. Mi - chael, row the boat a - shore, Hal - le - lu - jah.

Song 6: Skater's Waltz

New Notes

The new notes *B*, *C*, and *D* are introduced in this song. Figure A shows the staff and keyboard locations of these notes.

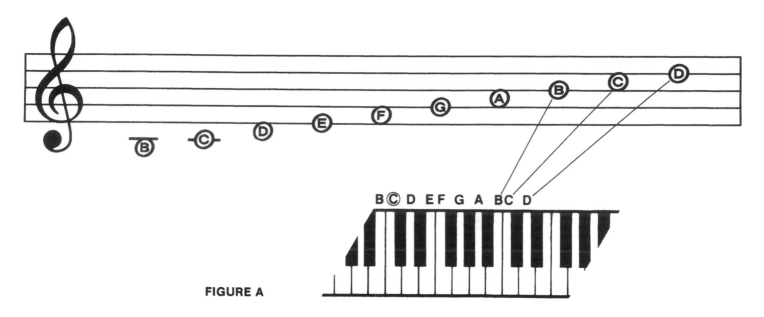

FIGURE A

The Octave

In Figure A, the new notes B, C, and D are eight notes higher than the B, C, and D you learned before. This span of eight notes is called an *OCTAVE*, which comes from the latin word for "eight."

Dotted-Half Notes

By adding a dot to a note, as shown in Figure B, the time value of the original note is increased by one-half. As you already know, a half note receives two beats. Half of two beats is one, or the equivalent of a quarter note. Therefore, a dotted half note is worth three beats.

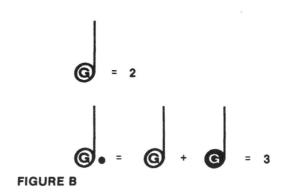

FIGURE B

A New Time Signature

Song number 6 uses a new time signature, 3/4. As you learned before, the 4 tells you the quarter note gets one beat. The upper number, 3, indicates three beats in each measure. This time signature indicates a rhythm commonly known as a *WALTZ*.

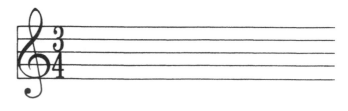

FIGURE C

Playing With the Waltz Rhythm

Press the WALTZ button in the rhythm section and press a chord key. You'll hear a repeating rhythm pattern of *ONE* heavy beat followed by *TWO* lighter beats. A portion of this pattern is illustrated in Figure D. As you listen to the rhythm, try to hear the melody of SKATER'S WALTZ in your mind.

FIGURE D

Each group of three beats starts with the heavier sound of the bass drum on the first beat and the cymbal on the second and third beats. The waltz pattern is often described by musicians as BOOM-chick-chick-BOOM-chick-chick as shown in Figure E.

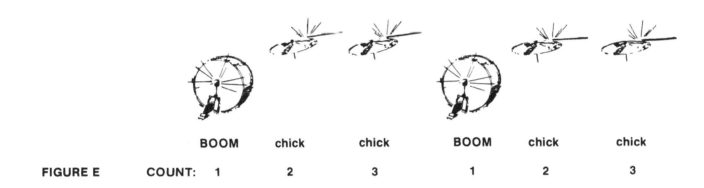

		BOOM	**chick**	**chick**	**BOOM**	**chick**	**chick**
FIGURE E	**COUNT:**	1	2	3	1	2	3

You'll also hear the deep sounds of the bass being played on the first beat and the chords being played on the second and third beats, as shown in Figure E.

FIGURE F

Skater's Waltz

Medium WALTZ

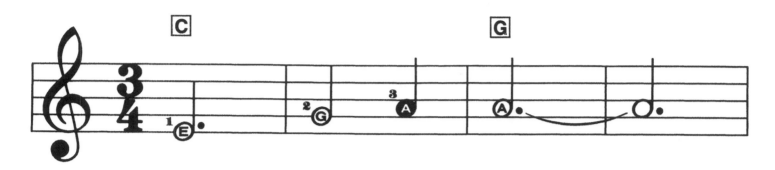

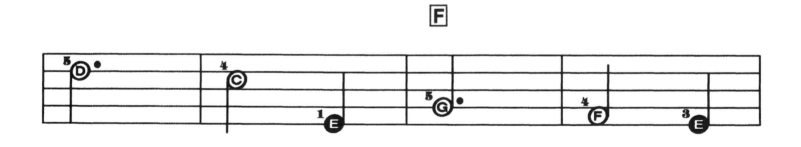

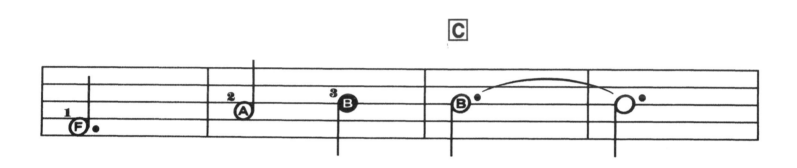

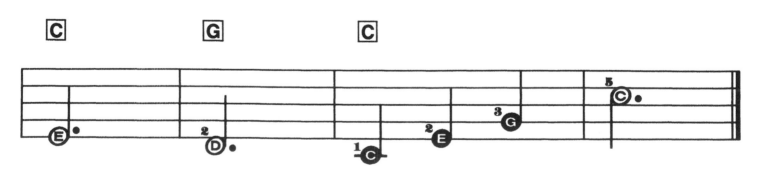

Song 7: Bring Back My Bonnie To Me

A New Note

This song introduces a new melody note, *E*. To make you're playing as smoothly as possible, be sure to follow the fingering suggestions on your music.

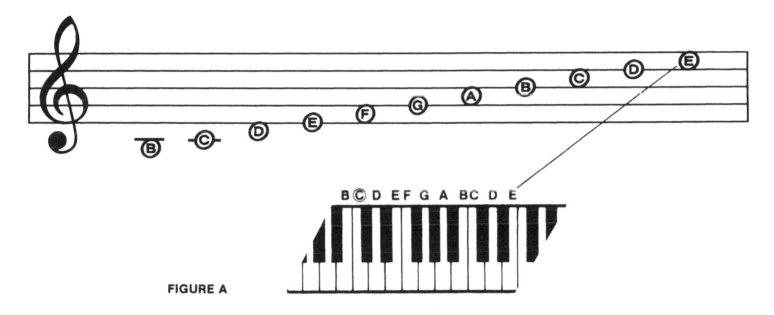

FIGURE A

A New Chord

Easy-Play

Consult your owner's guide for any instructions on playing seventh chords in this manner.

Forming Your Own Chords

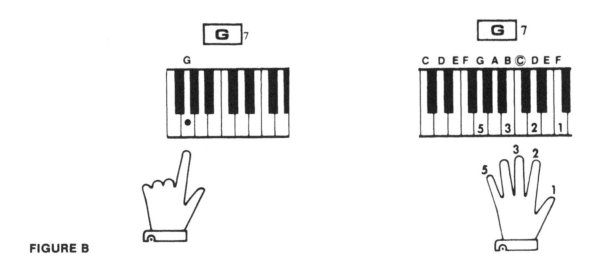

FIGURE B

Bring Back My Bonnie To Me

Medium fast WALTZ

BRIGHT 'N' BRASSY

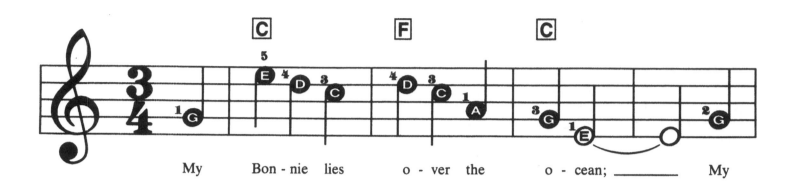

My Bon - nie lies o - ver the o - cean; _____ My

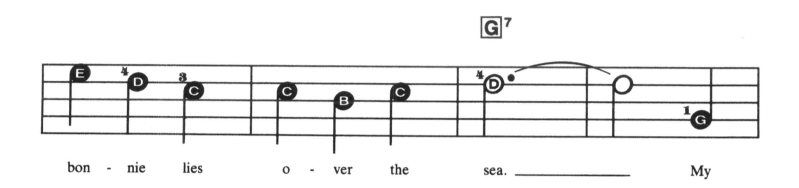

bon - nie lies o - ver the sea. _____ My

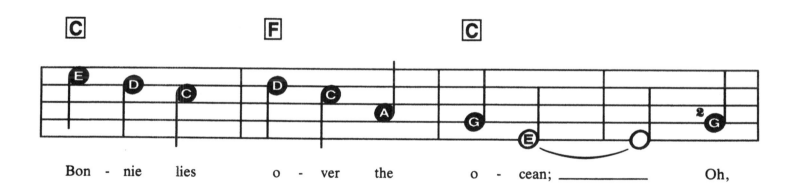

Bon - nie lies o - ver the o - cean; _____ Oh,

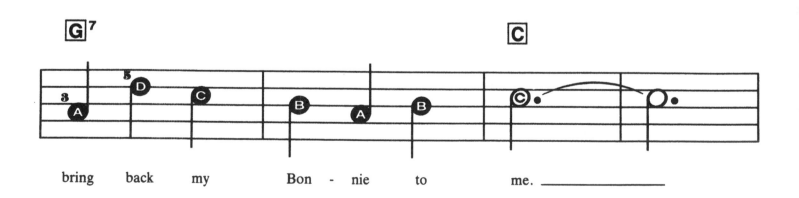

bring back my Bon - nie to me. _____

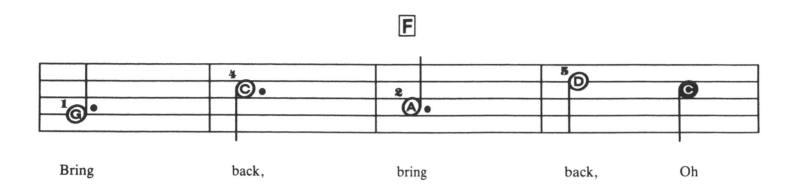

Bring   back,   bring   back,   Oh

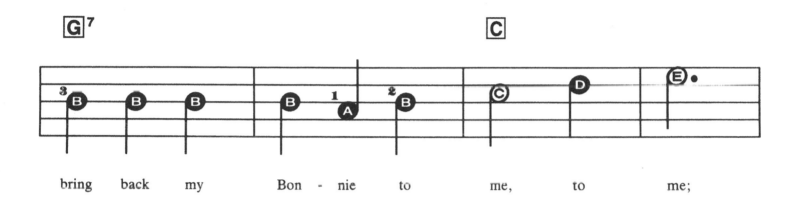

bring   back   my   Bon - nie   to   me,   to   me;

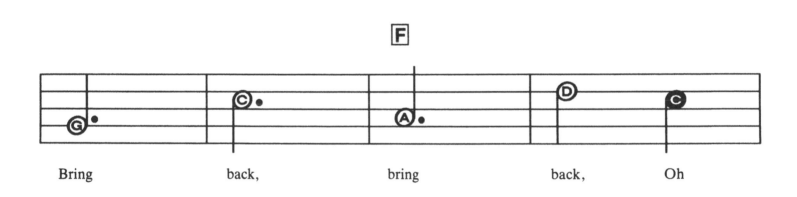

Bring   back,   bring   back,   Oh

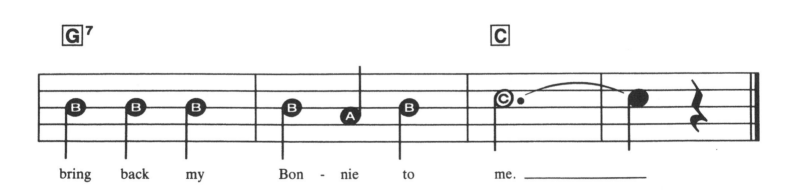

bring   back   my   Bon - nie   to   me. _____

Song 8: Du, Du, Liegst Mir Im Herzen

Medium fast WALTZ

FULL 'N' BRILLIANT

Du,   du   ligst   mir   im   Her - zen,

Du,   du   ligst   mir   im   Sinn.

Du,   du   machst   mir   viel   Schmer - zen,

Weiss   nicht,   wie   gut   ich   dir   bin?

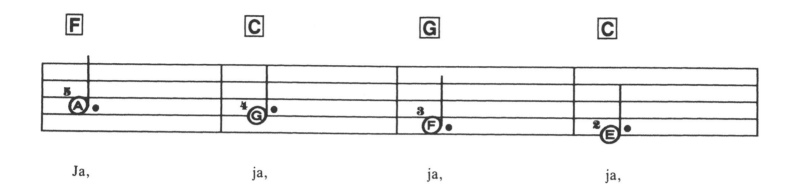

Ja,　　　　ja,　　　　ja,　　　　ja,

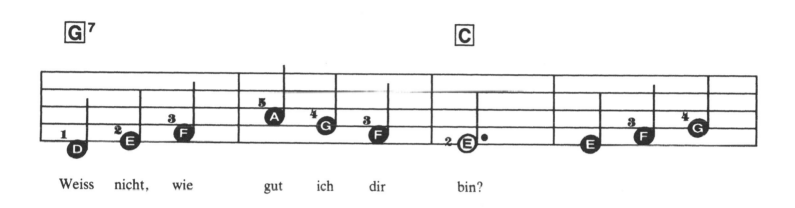

Weiss　nicht,　wie　gut　ich　dir　bin?

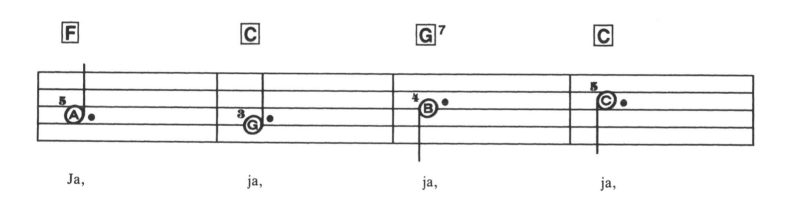

Ja,　　　　ja,　　　　ja,　　　　ja,

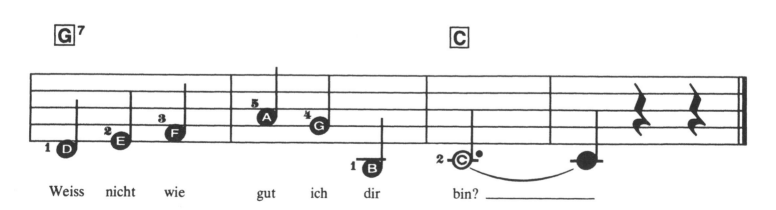

Weiss　nicht　wie　gut　ich　dir　bin? _____

Song 9: Red River Valley

Rests

A *REST* is a musical symbol that represents a period of silence. Rests have time values equal to their corresponding notes. Three kinds of rests are shown in Figure A.

A quarter note receives one beat.
A *QUARTER REST* (1) also receives one beat.

A half note receives two beats.
A *HALF REST* (2) receives two beats.
A whole note receives four beats.
A *WHOLE REST* (3) receives four beats, or equals one measure rest in $\frac{3}{4}$ time.

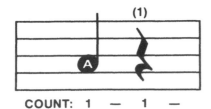

COUNT: 1 — 1 —

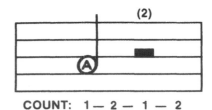

COUNT: 1 — 2 — 1 — 2

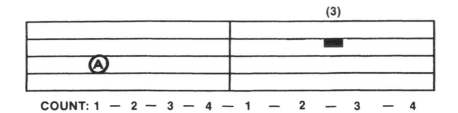

FIGURE A   COUNT: 1 — 2 — 3 — 4 — 1 — 2 — 3 — 4

Repeat Signs

Many musical arrangements require certain sections, or even the entire song, to be played twice. Instead of reprinting these sections, musical symbols called *REPEAT SIGNS* are used to indicate the section to be replayed.

Repeat signs appear most often in sets of two — one sign at the beginning of the section to be repeated, and one at the end. This is shown in Figure B.

When you come to the second repeat sign, go back to the first and repeat all of the measures between the two signs.

Occasionally you'll find only one repeat sign at the end of a section or a song, as shown in Figure C. Play to the sign, go back to the beginning of the song and play that section again. If there is more music after the repeat sign, just keep playing.

A song may also contain more than one set of repeat signs, as shown in Figure D.

When this occurs, play twice through all of the measures within the first set of repeat signs. Then, all of the measures within the second set should be played twice. In each case, always go back to the closest repeat sign.

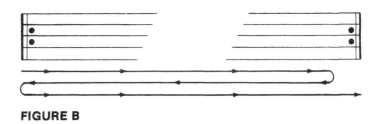

FIGURE B

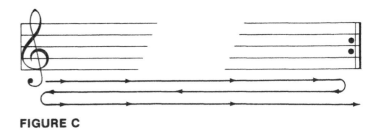

FIGURE C

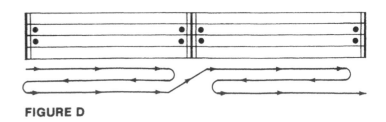

FIGURE D

Red River Valley

Medium FOX TROT or SWING

FULL 'N' MELLOW

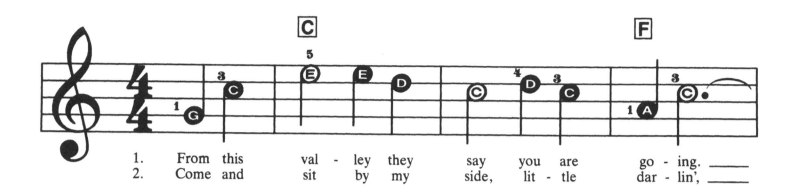

1. From this val - ley they say you are go - ing. _____
2. Come and sit by my side, lit - tle dar - lin', _____

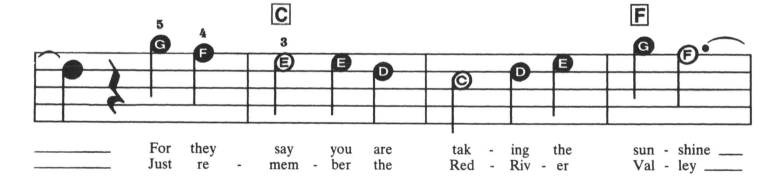

_____ We will miss your bright eyes and sweet smile, _____
_____ Do not has - ten to bid me a - dieu. _____

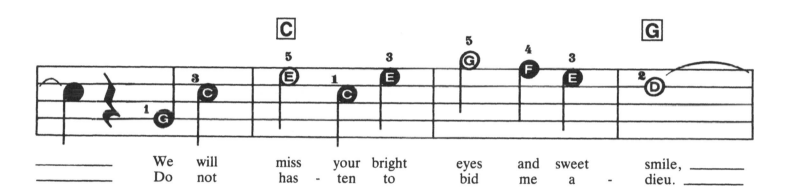

_____ For they say you are tak - ing the sun - shine _____
_____ Just re - mem - ber the Red - Riv - er Val - ley _____

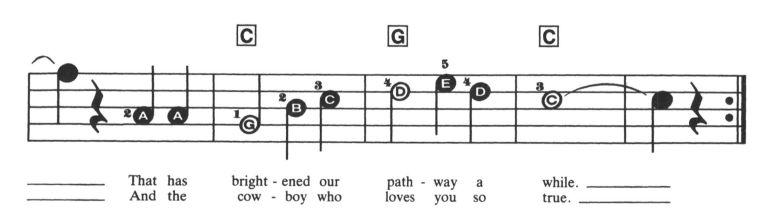

_____ That has bright - ened our path - way a while. _____
_____ And the cow - boy who loves you so true. _____

Song 10: Aloha Oe

A New Note

This song uses a new melody note, *F*. Figure A shownns its location on the keyboard and staff.

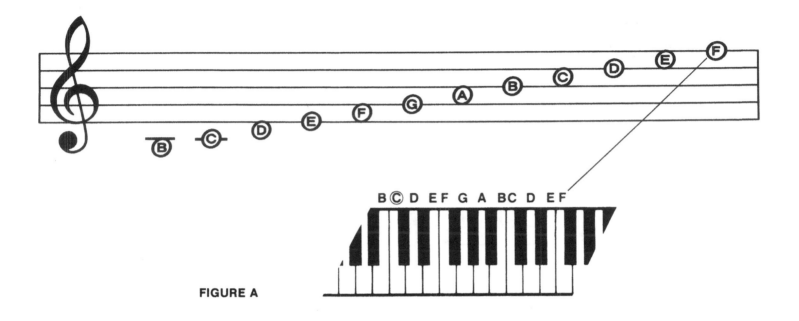

FIGURE A

Playing Double Notes in the Melody

In the songs to follow, the harmony notes are the ones that accompany, or harmonize with, the melody notes. If you wish to leave some of the harmony notes out, go right ahead. You can always add them later as you get a better feel for the song.

When you're playing more than one note at a time, different combinations of fingers must be used, depending upon the notes played and the relative movement of your right hand over the keyboard.

For your convenience and ease of playing, follow the suggested finger numbers next to the notes.Should a similar melodic pattern appear more than once in a song, only the first pattern indicates fingering.

If you enjoy playing double notes, you'll want to learn other things that can be done with the melodies of your favorite songs. Get your copy of "Fun With Melodies" from your dealer.

Aloha Oe

Medium FOX TROT

HAWAIIAN GUITAR
FULL 'N' MELLOW

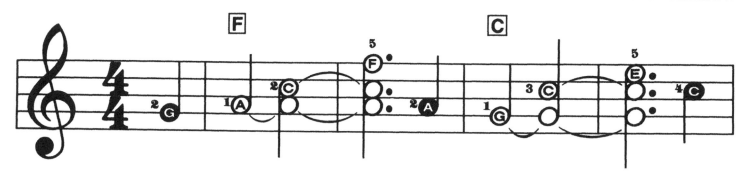

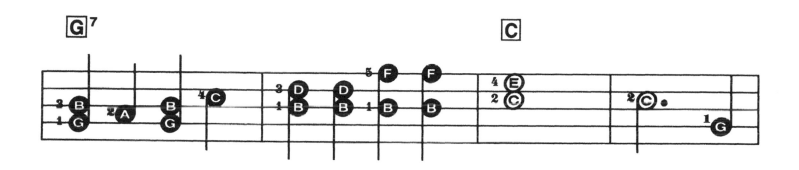

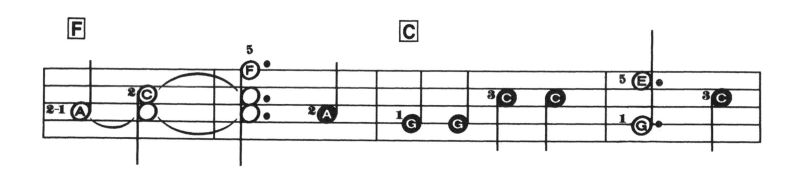

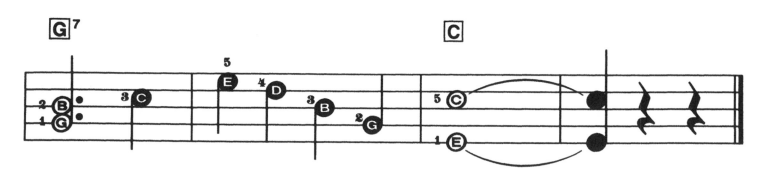

Song 11: Chopsticks

Double Endings

In Song 9, you learned about repeat signs. CHOPSTICKS contains a repeat sign in conjunction with another musical symbol, the *DOUBLE ENDING,* as shown in Figure A.

When you play CHOPSTICKS the first time, play the measures marked by the bracket with the number 1, the first ending. Play up to the repeat sign and return to the beginning. After playing the song a second time, skip the first ending (1) and play the measures marked by the bracket with the number 2, the second ending.

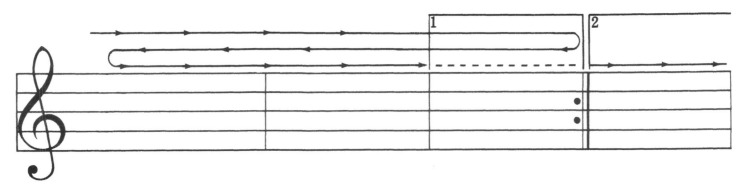

FIGURE A

Chopsticks

Medium fast WALTZ

BRIGHT 'N' BRASSY

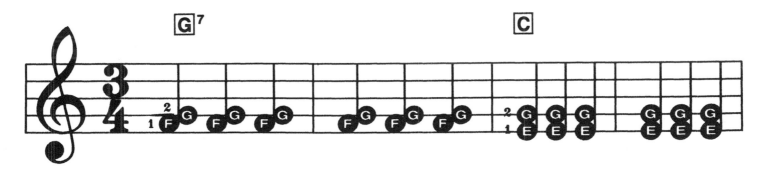

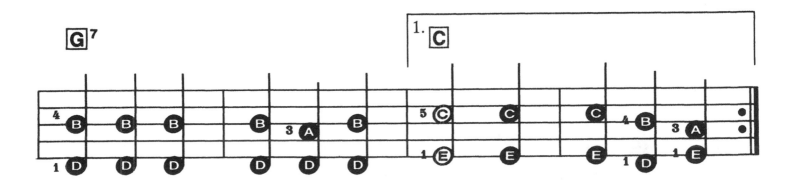

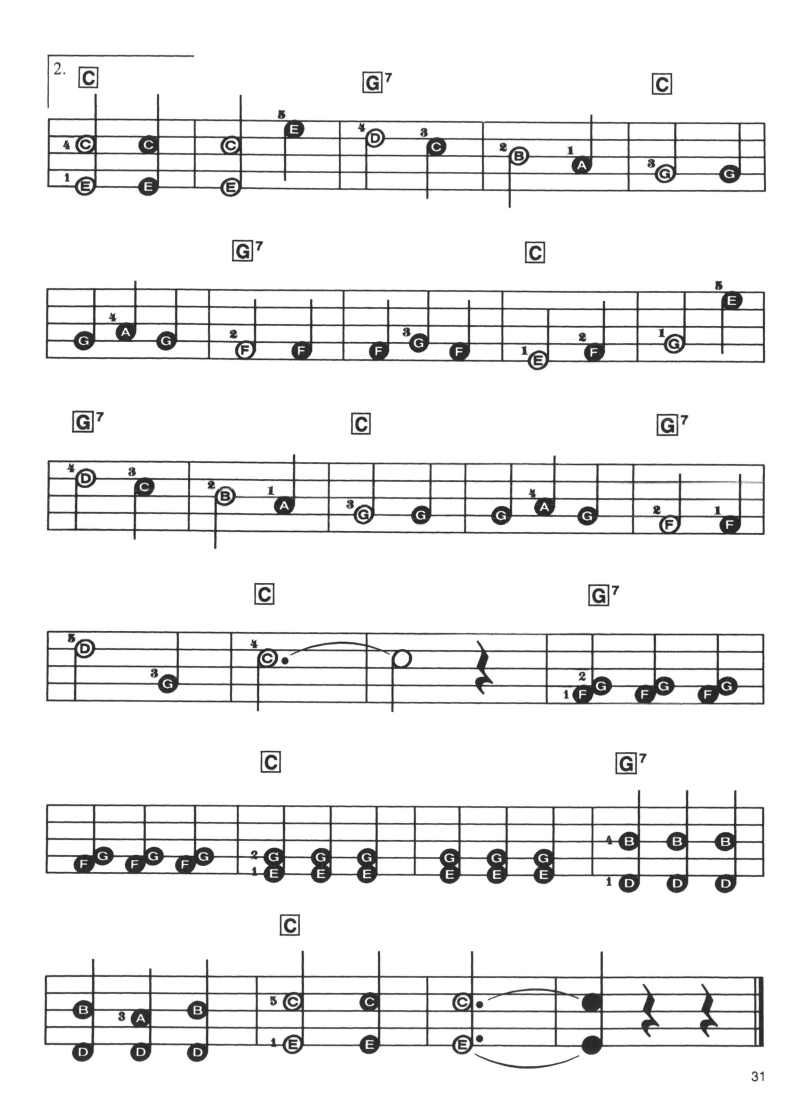

Song 12:Vive L'Amour

Medium Fast WALTZ

BIG 'N' BOLD

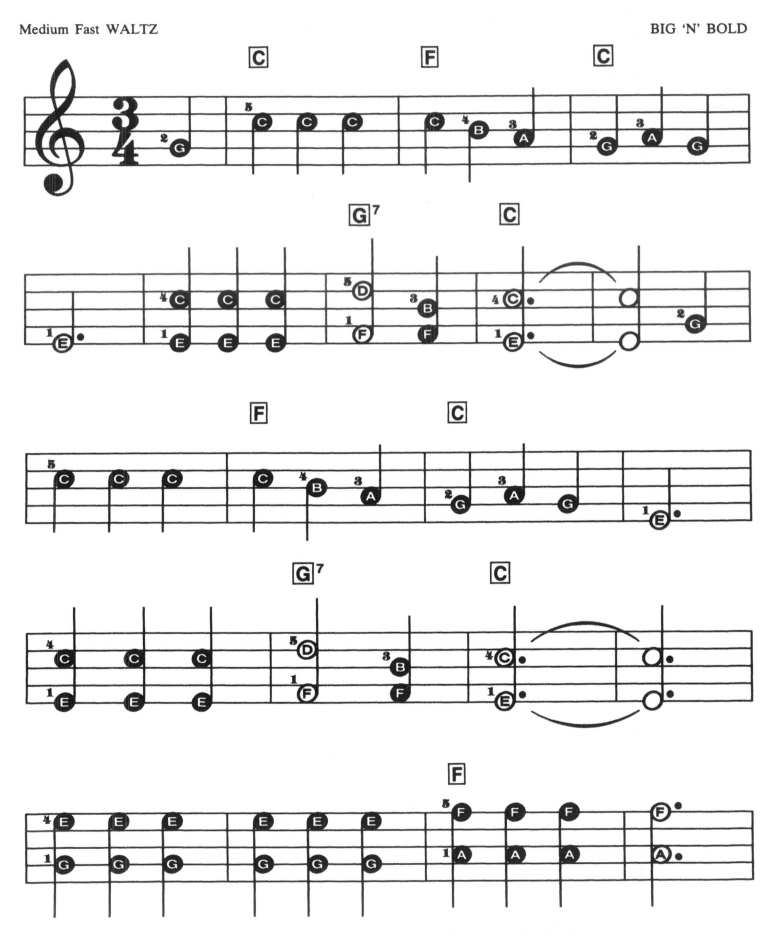

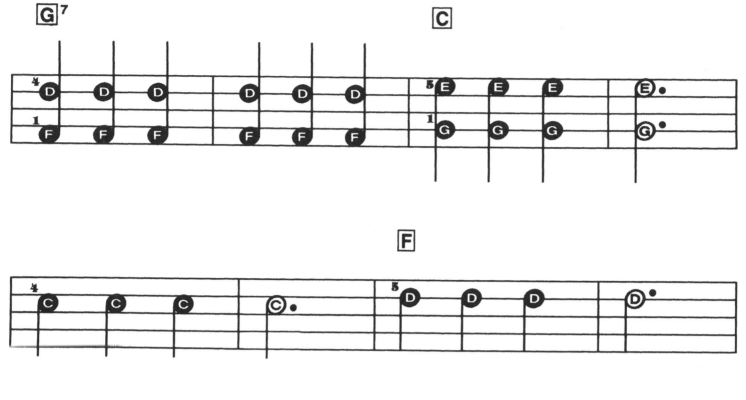

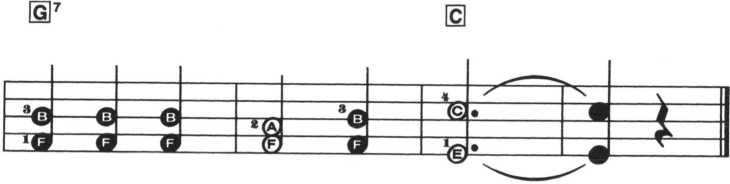

An Entire Library Is Available!

You can easily apply what you're learning in this book to many other songs. Thousands of tunes are available in our Easy Play series — top 40 hits, show tunes and TV themes, old standards, country favorites. See your dealer for these exciting, new collections.

While you're at it, ask about the other books in the Creative Playing series:

• EXPLORING AUTOMATIC FEATURES ON YOUR KEYBOARD — How to have fun using automatic rhythm, arpeggio feature, synchro-start, and fill-in (or drum break).

• CREATING SOUNDS ON YOUR KEYBOARD — Have fun learning what the voice and effect controls do, and how to use them. When to use special effects; how to use sounds to create moods.

• FUN WITH MELODIES — Create introductions and endings, phrase melodies with feeling, create "fills" and "turn arounds," basics of improvising.

• FUN WITH CHORDS — Start with easy-to-play, one-finger chords; learn to form your own. Create professional-sounding accompaniment by changing chord positions, using common tones, and harmonic continuity.

Song 13: Just A Closer Walk With Thee

This is the first song in which you'll be playing black keys, called *SHARPS* and/or *FLATS*. Before you learn about sharps and flats, however, it's important for you to understand *HALF-STEPS* and *WHOLE-STEPS*.

Half-Steps

A *HALF-STEP* is the distance between any two keys that are adjacent to one another and have no other key between them. There are three ways of forming half-steps, as shown in Figure A.

(1) From a white key to a black key.
(2) From a black key to a white key.
(3) From a white key to a white key.

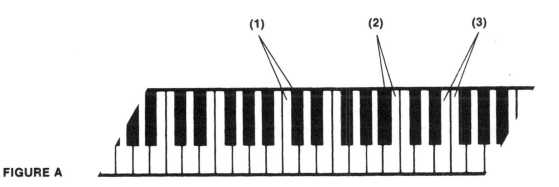

FIGURE A

Whole-Steps

Two half-steps equal one *WHOLE-STEP*. There are four ways of forming a whole-step, as shown in Figure B.

(4) From a white key to a white key, skipping a black key.
(5) From a black key to a black key, skipping a white key.

(6) From a white key to a black key, skipping a white key.
(7) From a black key to a white key, skipping a white key.

Figure B shows that there is always a middle key in a whole-step formation.

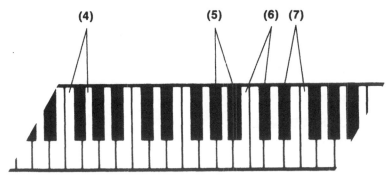

FIGURE B

Sharps and Flats

In this song, and future selections, you'll frequently see these signs (♯) (♭) appearing before certain notes on the staff. These signs are called *SHARPS* and *FLATS* and they're used to indicate tones that are to be raised or lowered one half-step.

♯ A *SHARP* tells you a tone should be raised one half-step.

♭ A *FLAT* tells you a tone should be lowered one half-step.

Figure C shows some sharped and flatted notes and their locations on the keyboard.

When a sharp or flat appears before a note in a given measure, it affects all the identical notes that follow in that measure.

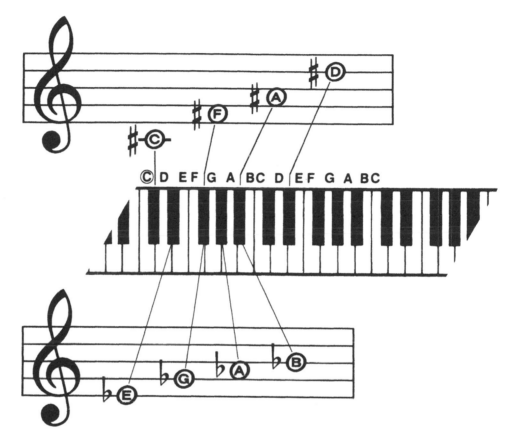

FIGURE C

Substitute Fingering

There are places in this song where you'll see two finger numbers near a single note (2-1) as shown in Figure D. These are called *SUBSTITUTE FINGERINGS* and merely tell you to press the key with the finger indicated by the first number; then, while holding it down, change to the finger indicated by the second number. This prepares your hand for the notes to follow.

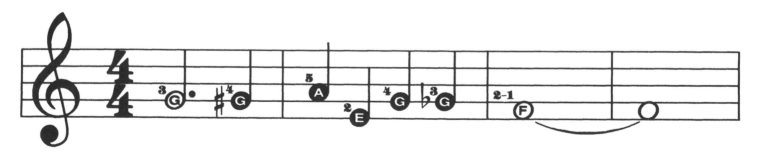

FIGURE D

Just A Closer Walk With Thee

Medium FOX TROT or SWING

FULL 'N' MELLOW

Song 14: Londonderry Air

A New Note

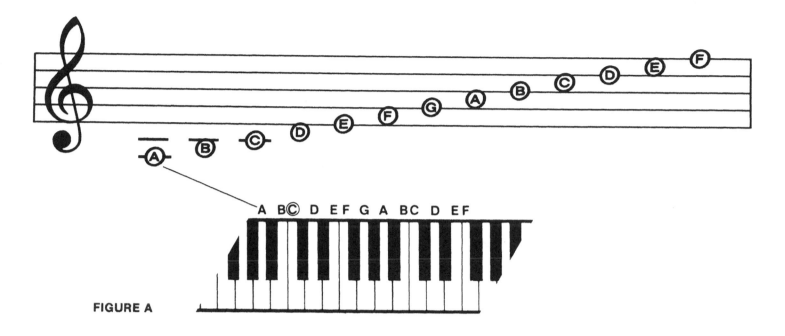

FIGURE A

Minor Chords

Consult your owner's manual for how easy-play minor chords are played on your particular instrument.

Figure B shows which keys to play if you form your own A-minor and F-minor chords.

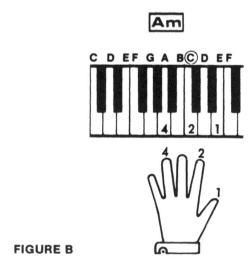

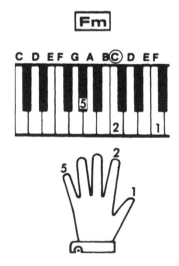

FIGURE B

At this point, you've learned about major, minor, and seventh chords. To learn how to REALLY use these chords, and others, pick up a copy of "Fun With Chords" — it's part of the Creative Playing Series.

Londonderry Air
(Popular Version Known As DANNY BOY)

Medium FOX TROT,
SWING or NO RHYTHM

SOFT SOLO

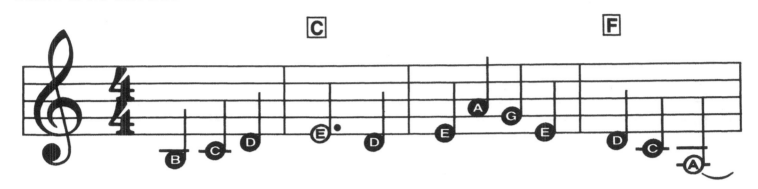

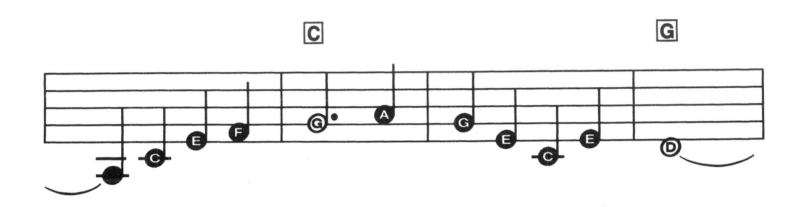

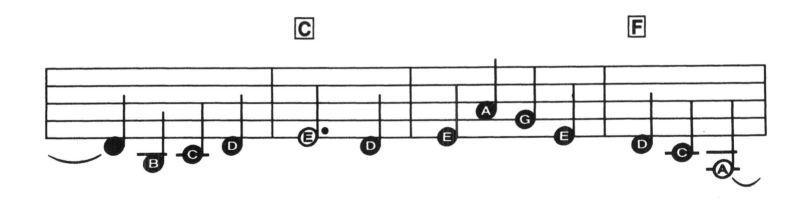

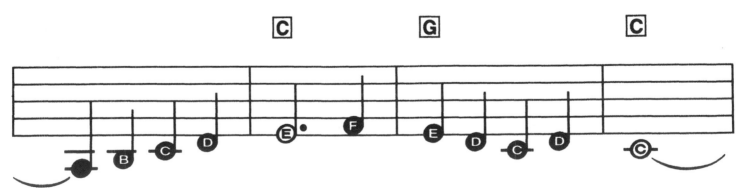

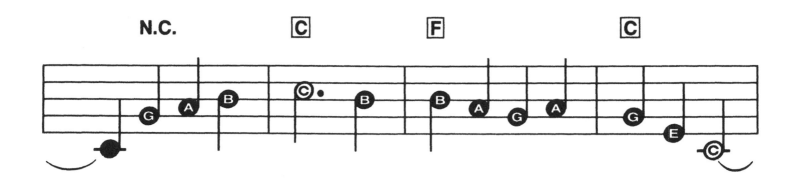

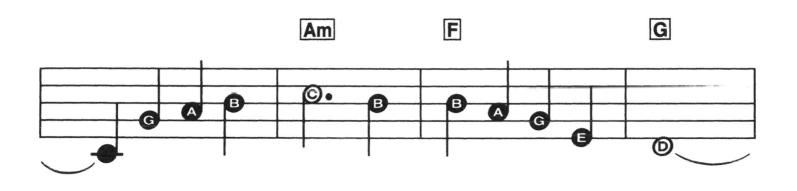

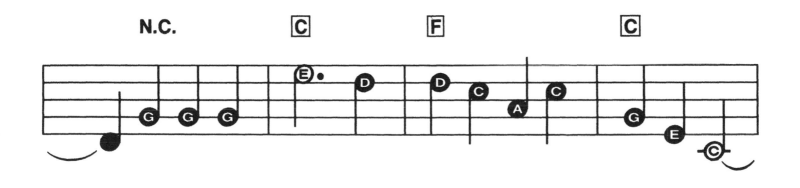

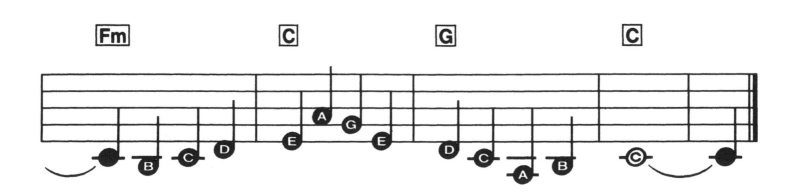

Song 15: The Jolly Coppersmith

A New Chord

Easy-Play

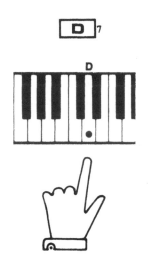

Forming Your Own Chords

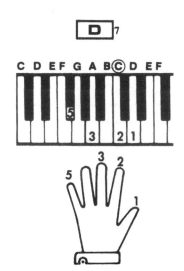

The Jolly Coppersmith

Medium POLKA, MARCH or FOX TROT

BRIGHT 'N' BRASSY

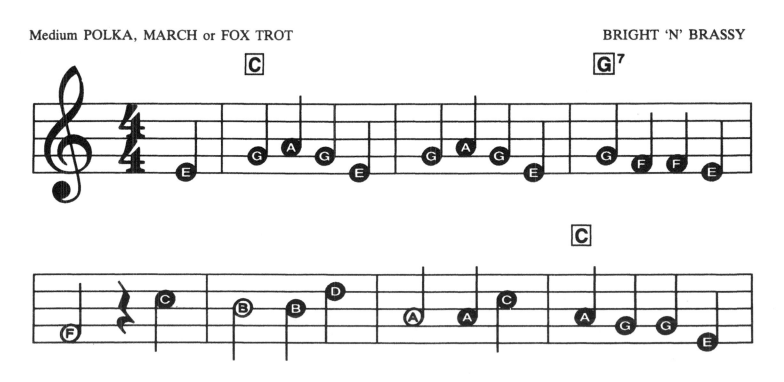

Song 16: Lavender's Blue

Eighth Notes

Up to now, you've been playing four different types of notes: whole, half, dotted-half, and quarter notes. Song 16 introduces the *EIGHTH NOTE*. These are what they look like.

FIGURE A

The time value of an eighth note is one half that of a quarter note. Therefore, two eighth notes are equal to one quarter note, as shown in Figure B.

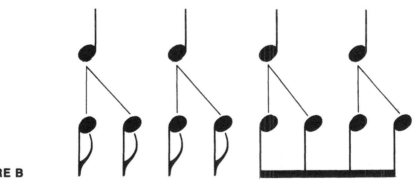

FIGURE B

The comments about time values on page 9 also apply to this material on eighth notes — just be aware of what they are. If you'd prefer to study them in detail, however, the material on the following page will be helpful.

Half Beats and Counting Eighth Notes

When you count eighth notes, each single beat must be divided into two equal parts, a *DOWNBEAT* and an *UPBEAT*. This can be more easily understood if you think about tapping your foot in time to music. Each foot-tap has two parts, a downbeat and an upbeat. For counting purposes, the downbeat is designated by a number, and the upbeat by the word "and" (&). All of this is illustrated in Figure C.

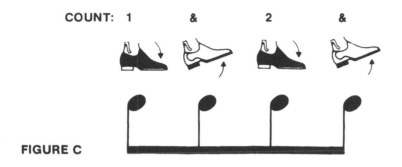

FIGURE C

Exercise in Eighth Notes

Practice the exercise below until you can play it smoothly and evenly, without hesitation. To help you play this first exercise, tap your foot and count aloud as you play.

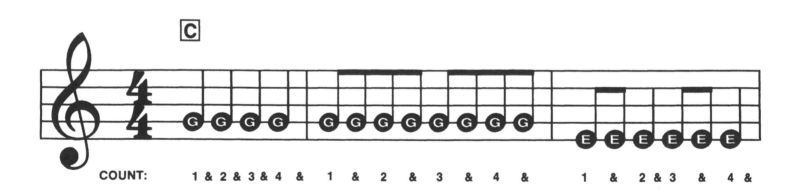

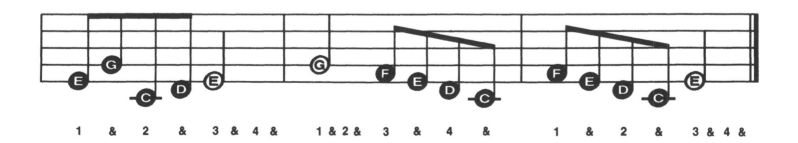

Lavender's Blue

Medium FOX TROT

FULL 'N' MELLOW

Master Chord Chart

Fingering is only a suggestion, based on these chord positions.

Keys used in each chord are named above chord symbol to guide you.

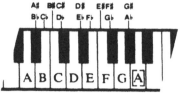

	C	**G**	**D**
MAJOR (chord letter only)	G-C-E **C** 5 2 1	G-B-D **G** 5 3 1	F#-A-D **D** 5 3 1
MINOR (m)	G-C-E♭ **Cm** 5 2 1	G-B♭-D **Gm** 5 3 1	F-A-D **Dm** 5 3 1
AUGMENTED (aug) (+)	C-E-G# **Caug** 5 3 1	G-B-D# **Gaug** 5 3 1	D-F#-A# **Daug** 5 3 1
SEVENTH (7)	G-B♭-C-E **C7** 5 3 2 1	G-B-D-F **G7** 5 3 2 1	F#-A-C-D **D7** 4 3 2 1
MINOR SEVENTH (m7)	G-B♭-C-E♭ **Cm7** 5 3 2 1	G-B♭-D-F **Gm7** 5 3 2 1	A-C-D-F **Dm7** 5 32 1
MAJOR SEVENTH (maj7) (M7)	C-E-G-B **Cmaj7** 5 3 2 1	G-B-D-F# **Gmaj7** 5 3 2 1	D-F#-A-C# **Dmaj7** 5 3 2 1
DIMINISHED (dim)	C-E♭-G♭-A **Cdim** 5 3 2 1	G-B♭-D♭-E **Gdim** 5 3 2 1	D-F-A♭-B **Ddim** 5 3 2 1

	A	E	B
MAJOR (chord letter only)	A-C#-E **A** — 4 2 1	G#-B-E **E** — 4 3 1	F#-B-D# **B** — 5 2 1
MINOR (m)	A-C-E **Am** — 4 2 1	G-B-E **Em** — 5 3 1	F#-B-D **Bm** — 5 2 1
AUGMENTED (aug) (+)	A-C#-F **Aaug** — 4 2 1 / 5 3 1	E-G#-C **Eaug** — 4 2 1 / 5 3 1	B-D#-G **Baug** — 4 2 1 / 5 3 1
SEVENTH (7)	G-A-C#-E **A7** — 54 2 1	G#-B-D-E **E7** — 4 3 2 1	F#-A-B-D# **B7** — 4 3 2 1
MINOR SEVENTH (m7)	G-A-C-E **Am7** — 54 2 1	G-B-D-E **Em7** — 5 3 21	F#-A-B-D **Bm7** — 4 3 2 1
MAJOR SEVENTH (maj7) (M7)	A-C#-E-G# **Amaj7** — 5 3 2 1	E-G#-B-D# **Emaj7** — 5 3 2 1	B-D#-F#-A# **Bmaj7** — 5 3 2 1
DIMINISHED (dim)	A-C-Eb-Gb **Adim** — 5 3 2 1	E-G-Bb-Db **Edim** — 5 3 2 1	B-D-F-Ab **Bdim** — 5 3 2 1

*Notes and keys having two names are called *enharmonic.* Detailed explanations are available in any music theory book.

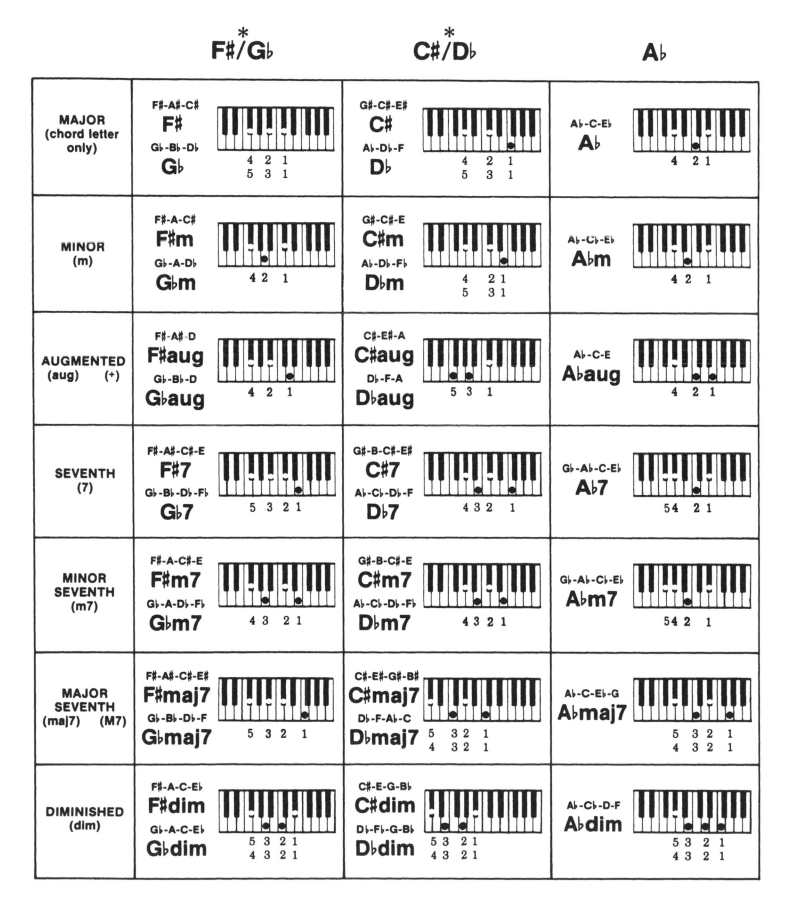

	Eb	Bb	F
MAJOR (chord letter only)	G-Bb-Eb **Eb** — 5 3 1	Bb-D-F **Bb** — 4 2 1	A-C-F **F** — 4 2 1
MINOR (m)	Gb-Bb-Eb **Ebm** — 5 3 1	Bb-Db-F **Bbm** — 4 2 1	Ab-C-F **Fm** — 4 2 1
AUGMENTED (aug) (+)	Eb-G-B **Ebaug** — 4 2 1	Bb-D-F# **Bbaug** — 5 3 1 / 4 2 1	F-A-C# **Faug** — 5 3 1 / 4 2 1
SEVENTH (7)	G-Bb-Db-Eb **Eb7** — 5 3 21	F-Ab-Bb-D **Bb7** — 5 32 1	A-C-Eb-F **F7** — 5 3 2 1
MINOR SEVENTH (m7)	Gb-Bb-Db-Eb **Ebm7** — 5 3 21	Ab-Bb-Db-F **Bbm7** — 5 4 2 1 / 4 3 2 1	Ab-C-Eb-F **Fm7** — 5 3 2 1 / 4 3 2 1
MAJOR SEVENTH (maj7) (M7)	Eb-G-Bb-D **Ebmaj7** — 5 3 2 1	Bb-D-F-A **Bbmaj7** — 5 3 2 1	F-A-C-E **Fmaj7** — 5 3 2 1
DIMINISHED (dim)	Eb-Gb-A-C **Ebdim** — 4 3 2 1	Bb-Db-Fb-G **Bbdim** — 4 3 2 1	F-Ab-Cb-D **Fdim** — 5 3 2 1